Owl Gulch Elegies

poems by

Peter Waldor

Finishing Line Press
Georgetown, Kentucky

Also by Peter Waldor

Door to a Noisy Room
The Wilderness Poetry of Wu Xing
Who Touches Everything
The Unattended Harp
State of the Union
Gate Posts with No Gate
Nice Dumpling

Owl Gulch
Elegies

Copyright © 2020 by Peter Waldor
ISBN 978-1-64662-120-0 First Edition
All rights reserved under International and Pan-American Copyright Conventions. No part of this book may be reproduced in any manner whatsoever without written permission from the publisher, except in the case of brief quotations embodied in critical articles and reviews.

ACKNOWLEDGMENTS

Thanks to the following journals where some of these poems first appeared:

Badlands
Main Street Rag
Montrose Mirror

Elegy for Glider Bob was made into a broadside by the *Letterpress Depot*.

Publisher: Leah Maines
Editor: Christen Kincaid
Cover Art: Peter Waldor
Author Photo: Melissa Plantz
Cover Design: Elizabeth Maines McCleavy

Printed in the USA on acid-free paper.
Order online: www.finishinglinepress.com
also available on amazon.com

Author inquiries and mail orders:
Finishing Line Press
P. O. Box 1626
Georgetown, Kentucky 40324
U. S. A.

Table of Contents

Lanterns 1

Kiss of Death 2

Hidden Sign 3

Teacher 6

Splayed Cairns 7

Common Sense 8

Extra Layers 9

Old Climber 10

Elegy for Charlotte Fox 11

Sour Dough Starter 13

Orphan Camel Colt 14

Last Dollar Saloon 15

Memorial Shrine 16

Elegy for Doctor David 17

Brightness 20

Finally Turning Back 21

No More Humans 22

Elegy for Glider Bob 23

Volunteers 25

Old Married Couple 27

Green Gentian Stalk 28

Lanterns

Piles of fresh yellow
bear scat light my way
down the mountain
past dusk I forgot
my light so thank god
for the dim fecal
lanterns keeping me
off cliff bands and slides
A passing thought
I could eat the berries
in the scat if I had to
A passing thought
I am closing
in on the beast
Every few yards
a fresh pile
Given the shapeliness
and luminescence
of the berries
buckthorn I think
it seems there was
very little digestion
not much help for
the looming hibernation

Kiss of Death

Back at tree line a wolf
hops to and fro
like a child at the end
of a pier. My partner,
as usual, way ahead,
tinkling up the talus
like a pianist.
Not long enough
since she tried to take
her own life but just
missed that French kiss.
What if she goes
over the knife edge?
What if by accident?
What if this sacred mountain
has nothing to do
with healing suffering?
What if she didn't love Edith Piaf?
At least, on top,
she was breathing hard.
She squeezed my arm.
At least she signed
the summit register
in her U.S. Cyrillic script
and left a goofy line
from Lao Tzu
about governing being
like frying small fish.
O dear impossibility
of friendship!

Hidden Sign

Blue bells
just buds
unnoticed

going up
the mountain
blossoms
going down

A steel sign
at the Deer Tail
Basin and Ballard

Mountain Trail
junction
Two drooping rusty
arrows Deer Tail

left Ballard right
How fanciful
to hide

a marker where
so few go
Blue bells
just buds

The popping
of the welder's torch
talus sliding

The welder
took big risks
in the mountains
Once he evaded

park rangers
and made a first
free ascent

at Ship Rock
Then he died
of a disease
The arrows at

the end of the sign
could be drooping
hands on a cross
It was a good job

in the empire
to harvest oak
for crosses

in the dense
Massimina Forest
The woodsmen pair
could spend

tranquil days
above Rome
with their

two man saw
Blossoms
going down

It's no god welded
on the junction sign
but a street urchin
caught taking

a round of bread
Blue bells
just buds

Teacher

He died in an avalanche
while teaching
avalanche awareness
When he coiled his
Black Diamond rope
if it ended in 23 coils
he flaked it apart
and started over
Once he confided
that though he loved
his loved ones
he loved most
of all the feeling
when he left them
and he was alone
reflecting on their
time together
Say all his gear
was in his truck
with its weak lights
and rusted carriage
and he was driving west
to Indian Creek
where a climber can
slip all the way
into a crack
like a flower
between pages

Splayed Cairns

A ranger friend
was fired when
the Forest Service
discovered she was
scattering trail cairns
in the wilderness.
They didn't understand
her kindness and how
she only wanted to help
us to find our own way.
You may find her high up,
with no water gourd,
her poncho always
smells of smoke,
her head
an eternal flame.
If you get lucky
she may stop to
talk weather.

Common Sense

Common sense dictates
as I get deeper in wilderness
any trail will thin and vanish
leaving only animal paths, if that.
But I found a trail that
the further in -- the further away
from civilization -- the truer it becomes.
I still follow, though it goes
away from everything I know,
so remote even the lichens
converse without inhibitions
in their gravelly sopranos.

Extra Layers

A friend was found near
death, hypothermic,
above Owl Gulch.
Her big pack had pants,
hat, extra jackets and
an emergency blanket
all stowed like an
axe in a glass case.
She could not explain.

Old Climber

The fifth leg
of the spider's
eight legs
pressed the snow
and the avalanche
let go...
Meanwhile
the old climber
was so slow
groaning up
the switchbacks
skis lashed to
her rucksack
she made it
for the aftermath
and not her burial
She lifted a shattered
pine limb to her face
and inhaled the ichor

Elegy for Charlotte Fox

1
The secret to extreme mountain exploration
is to suffer unduly and then to feel
better even as conditions worsen.
Charlotte mastered this art.

2
During difficult moments she would simply
say she helped out and was helped.

3
Given her 8,000-meter resume
it was hard to say hello when
our paths' crossed on Tomboy Road.
Did fame make her lonely?

4
Charlotte was private as a marmot,
but at base camps she would treat
the whole expedition to local brews,
and if you pulled her aside she'd
listen patiently to your story.

5
Her brief essay on her Everest climb
was a reproof to the best seller.
She said, in essence, Everest
is a sport climb for rich tourists,
mistakes were made, people died,
there is nothing more to say.

6
Someone pinned a sprig of lilac
between wiper and windshield
on her giant red expedition van.
Some will know why it is there.
Others will wonder why,
and some won't notice a thing
before her distant family
takes the van away.

Sour Dough Starter

A favorite aunt cleaned
her fridge after the accident
keeping the Dijon and Coke
not noticing the white jar
of sour dough starter
blending in with the door
passed down 400 years
200 in Holland 200
in the "new" world
Once she baked loaves
for her friends after
a day of jam cracks
at Indian Creek
What will the next tenant
make of the jar
in the empty fridge
Will they do what
I would and toss it
quickly or will they smell
its old bandage stink
and honor the tradition

Orphan Camel Colt

A good friend
of the missing climber
didn't volunteer with
Search and Rescue
and their eighty
person team sweeping
the scree and forest
Instead she searched
on her own ever higher
All she found above
Owl Gulch was an
orphan camel colt
no brand braid or bell
its humps sagging

Last Dollar Saloon

A young climber
hoped to learn
others had died
on Lizard Head
before he climbed it
so when he
recounted his climb
at the Last Dollar
he could tell
the history

Memorial Shrine

Deep in wilderness I found
a memorial shrine
smooth stones and a dish
The incense embers long since
blown and washed away
Who carried it so high
and deep in the backcountry
Must the sage be gone
Can I never ask a question

Elegy for Doctor David

1
Nothing lives long
Nothing lives long
Nothing lives long
Not even the mountains,
chanted David's friends
at his cave.

2
Chanted White Antelope before
his murder at Sand Creek.

3
David had no money but
rented the Sheridan Opera House
for $500 and for twenty minutes,
in his silk wizard robe recited
his silent poem, long before
composers discovered silence.

4
Who doesn't have a son with long hair?
When Absalom stole David's concubines
and declared himself King, he was undone
when his hair caught in a branch.
We would call it a bouffant, and while stuck
he was killed with three darts to his heart.

5
Wise move for David to leave Baltimore
and sojourn in Bear Creek where
his dreads grayed to his waist
and bears in nearby caves
never bothered him as he
practiced spirit healing.

6
Great caves are hard to enter
and hard to leave. David's friends
clawed up the cliffs to his cave
where he surveyed the wild
from his loam balcony.
His mattress, stove pipe, and healing
stones were all gone, just David's
silent poem and White Antelope's song.

7
White Antelope said the earth and the
mountains remain but David's friends
said they also don't live long.

8
How irate David was when someone
called him "Black David" in his presence.

9
David never wrestled angels,
just walked barefoot with Mother Earth
and changed his name to Michal.

10
He was the Rainbow Gathering's
official healer, though they
abhorred all officials.
He drove their bus up Bear Creek
before the land was preserved and an
iron bar placed across the access trail.

11
David was inconsolable after Absalom's death
and hid in a cave where people found
him and begged him to return.

12
Just four or five people that night at the Sheridan.
David also had a radio show and once,
for an hour, played the sound of old shoes
walking down old stairs.

13
A friend of David's lost $500 in the wilderness
and though it was years later it was the $500
David used to rent the Sheridan.

14
David, your passing leaves us with no healer,
and White Antelope's children aren't
with us to chant against injustice.

15
At first, during the twenty-minute
silent poem, the audience fidgeted
and sighed but then relaxed as if
a great weight was gone though
the weight of the world was still there.

Brightness

All day in the wilderness
at night a squatter
in this lonely hut
I sweep with its broken broom
No carved name on a rafter
Some shavings
a gut string and a file
perhaps a luthier
was last here
Moon brighter than sun
As much as I dream
of living with animals
I love the hard cot
and broken window

Finally Turning Back

but taking a mental
picture of where to go
next time deeper
into the wilderness
next time until I bring
that picture to my grave
where it will be proudly
displayed in the great
Earth album

No More Humans

No more humans
but animals
keep an old
human trail intact
The quadrupeds are
masters of the elegy
Their paws drum
the earth
old fingers on
an oak table

Elegy for Glider Bob

1
The day after he died, my son and I biked
near the crash site, high up, we stopped to rest
and in a hail storm found a patch of chanterelles,
the mother lode, we harvested in somber glee,
as I had unwanted thoughts about the cycle
of life and decomposition.

2
Just through the clearing Bob's plane
was strapped to a flatbed truck,
minus wings, the fuselage was intact,
no crumpling near the cockpit.
It was a trespass to see the wreck.

3
For all those years I thought I would wait
until I had a terminal illness, to give Bob
some glider business, but I had changed
my mind and was about to sign up.
After all, he had been gliding for 34 years.

4
Four times I remember being on a peak
and Bob buzzing us, buzz is the wrong word,
whispered. I remember him smiling and waving.
That's a lie, but he did tilt a wing.

5
Before the last town council election there was
a banner in front of the market "Anyone but Bob!"
What a credit to his vision, to inspire critics so.

6.
May 1, 2001, Bob played Mr. Cellophane
in a town park production of Chicago,
before the end there was an epic
hail storm and no one left.

7.
Who knew Bob made children's furniture?
His old friend took a mortised spindle
that Bob discarded. Now it's leaning
on the friend's wall. It is not needed
 to remind him of Bob. It will stay
there until his own time to go.

8.
Bob rode his hulking antique chrome Harley
with laughing finesse in the July fourth parade,
stars and stripes painted on head and face.
He fought for affordable housing.

9.
Fly quietly.
Unmade friend.

Volunteers

Beautiful day and the eighty odd
search and rescue volunteers
were sweeping a new section
of forest fifty feet apart but
meeting frequently and talking
of many things some feeling
guilty for the glee they felt being
out in the summer wilderness
Since so many days had passed
and still no sign the rumors
were wild a few were saying
it was a life insurance scam
and he was relaxing on a beach
in Mexico where his wife would
join him someday when he was
forgotten and others said
he was on the same beach
with a lover but I believed the talk
that he was killed and dragged
to a cave by a mountain lion
so we couldn't find his body
though it would be better
for his children if he were
still alive even under
suspicious circumstances
And when the search party
dwindled to a few old friends
an airplane finally saw the body
just outside the search zone
When they reached his remains
they found his glass jar
of pine patch salve cracked
the salve dripping on the scree
Who knows if anyone felt
ashamed for talk of lovers
and life insurance

Do they hang their heads
passing his wife on Main Street
Are they disappointed
he died doing what he loved
even though they know
there are no good deaths

Old Married Couple

Every other day or so
walking the hard way
up Tomboy Road to the
long decommissioned
Savage Basin mines,
skins leathered
beautifully by lifetimes
above tree lines.
The chorus line of old legs.
Talking or not talking.
If you corner them
she won't say a thing
and he cheerfully
won't say much.
He won't say how
he lost his right arm,
one safety pin holding
the starched sleeve of his
rancher holiday shirt.
Seasons already
since we met
on the miners' road,
just a coincidence
the seep by
the big turn is dry
now even in spring.

Green Gentian Stalk

Not easy for
a flower to give
birth to a flower
Brittle ruin
dead but erect
after waiting
70 years
to bloom
Seeds trapped
in seed cases
dice in a casino cup

Peter **Waldor** is the author of eight books of poetry, including *Door to a Noisy Room* which won the Kinereth Gensler Award from Alice James Books; *Who Touches Everything*, which won the National Jewish Book Award and *Gate Posts with No Gate*, which is a collaboration with a group of visual artists.

Waldor was the Poet Laureate of San Miguel County, Colorado from 2014 to 2015. His work has appeared in many journals, including the *American Poetry Review, Ploughshares, the Iowa Review, the Colorado Review, Poetry Daily, Verse Daily, Fungi Magazine* and *Mothering Magazine.* He lives in Trout Lake, Colorado.

www.ingramcontent.com/pod-product-compliance
Lightning Source LLC
LaVergne TN
LVHW041516070426
835507LV00012B/1622